Way of the Cross—
Way of Justice

Way of the Cross—
Way of Justice

Leonardo Boff

*Translated from the Portuguese
by John Drury*

ORBIS BOOKS
Maryknoll, New York 10545

The Catholic Foreign Mission Society of America (Maryknoll) recruits and trains people for overseas missionary service. Through Orbis Books Maryknoll aims to foster the international dialogue that is essential to mission. The books published, however, reflect the opinions of their authors and are not meant to represent the official position of the society.

Library of Congress Cataloging in Publication Data

Boff, Leonardo.
    Way of the Cross-way of justice.

    Translation of Via-Sacra da justiça.
    1. Jesus Christ—Crucifixion—Meditations.   2. Christianity and justice—Meditations.   I. Title.
    BT450.B5713   232   79-23776
    ISBN 0-88344-701-0

First published as *Via-sacra da justiça*, copyright © 1978 by Editora Vozes Ltda., Rua Fre: Luís, 100, 25.600 Petrópolis, RJ, Brazil

English translation copyright © 1980 by Orbis Books, Maryknoll, NY 10545

Contents

Introduction

Theology seeks to be a rational, grammatically organized discourse about the faith. It is born of the concrete experience of faith, and it should nurture that faith. The ultimate criterion determining the truth of any and all theology is whether it produces a life of faith, hope, and charity. Theology is true insofar as it is translated into meditation, prayer, conversion, the following of Christ, and commitment to our fellow human beings. If a theology does not lead people to take that step, that is a sure sign that it is a pharaonic, courtesan theology, an activity of religious scribes who are in the service, not of God, but of the court and the power of the gods of this world.

For years now I have been working on the mystery of Christ in theological terms. I have considered his cosmic dimension (*O evangelho do Cristo cósmico*, 1971); his life and message of liberation (*Jesus Cristo Liberatador*, 1972; Eng. trans., *Jesus Christ Liberator*, Maryknoll, N.Y.: Orbis Books, 1979); his resurrection as the ground of our hope (*A ressurreição de Cristo e a nossa na morte*, 1973); his violently enforced and freely accepted death (*Paixão de Cristo, paixão do mundo*, 1977); and finally his redemptive and glorifying incarnation (*Encarnação: jovialidade e humanidade de nosso Deus*, 1976).

In the light of the perspectives and convictions acquired over the course of seven years of christological studies, I now present this Way of the Cross, which is meant to be a prayerful theology or a theological prayer.

Theology is *ante et retro oculata*: it has two eyes. One looks back toward the past, where salvation broke in; the other looks toward the present, where salvation becomes reality here and now. If theology were to look with only one eye, it would suffer from myopia. It would merely be either an archeology of the past or a phenomenology of the present. To look with both eyes is to be capable of accepting the import of the past while at the same time creating a meaning for the present.

This Way of the Cross seeks to use both eyes of theology. It is a Way of the Cross, with one eye focusing on the historical Jesus: his life, condemnation, death, and resurrection. It is also a Way of Justice, its other eye focusing on the Christ of faith who continues his passion today in his brothers and sisters who are being condemned, tortured, and killed for the cause of justice.

Viewed historically, the passion of Jesus was the result of his message of universal liberation and of his attitudes that threatened the prevailing order of his day. He stood up for a justice, a righteousness, greater than that of the Pharisees: the justice of the kingdom of God. The various authorities got together to eliminate "the Holy and Just One" (Acts 3:14). They were actors in a drama that went much deeper than they themselves. The real protagonists were the Evil One and the sin of the world; they were the ones ultimately responsible for Jesus' death.

Viewed theologically, the passion of Jesus was the consequence of his fidelity to his Father and his fellow human beings. In the face of human rejection, the Father did not cease to will his kingdom and to press for its establishment even now in this world, even though that would entail the criminal elimination of his own Son. Given the sinful condition of the world, Jesus would have to die if he wanted to be obedient and loyal to his Father. Despite rejection by human beings, the kingdom triumphed through the sacrifice of Jesus, who accepted his sacrifice in selfless freedom rather than fatalistically.

Today the passion of the mystical Christ, embodied in the lives of those who are sacrificed for the cause of justice, preserves the same structure as the passion of the historical Jesus. Like Jesus, many people today are being persecuted and killed for defending the rights of the lowly and the just claims of the poor. They suffer this fate out of fidelity to God, who asks them to sacrifice their lives for those causes. Those causes are greater than life itself, because they are the causes of God and God's kingdom. These people prefer the glory of a violent death to the joy of an accursed freedom, as a Christian martyr of the third century put it.

The resurrection of the crucified Jesus proves that the sacrifice of one's life out of love for the downtrodden and abused is not meaningless. It means sharing in the fullness of life and the definitive triumph of justice. The Crucified One is the Living One. Those who are crucified today will also live.

This Way of the Cross seeks to transmute these truths into prayer and meditation.

Way of the Cross—
Way of Justice

Jesus is condemned to death

> *At this they shouted,*
> *"Away with him! Away with him!*
> *Crucify him!" . . .*
> *In the end, Pilate handed Jesus over to*
> *be crucified (John 19:15–16).*

Then:
Jesus was condemned to death

J esus was captured at night,
taken away by soldiers,
stripped of his garments,
interrogated,
tortured,
crowned with sharp thorns,
and finally condemned to death on a cross
by Pontius Pilate,
the representative of Roman imperial authority.
But why was Jesus condemned to death?
Hadn't the people exclaimed:
"He has done everything well!
He makes the deaf hear and the mute speak!"
(Mark 7:37)?

Jesus announced the nearness of the Kingdom
(or Reign) of God.

That meant that the complete, definitive liberation
of humankind and the world
was at hand.
Jesus' miracles demonstrated this clearly.
This liberation, which brings
life,
grace,
justice,
love,
and peace,
begins with those most in need of it:
the poor,
who are treated unjustly by the rich;
the sick,
who are thrust off to the margins of society;
and sinners,
who are expelled from the precincts of religion.

Access to this liberation granted by God
is not achieved by a mere wave of some magic wand.
People must undergo a conversion,
must change their way of thinking and acting.
Only to those who undergo conversion
is the Kingdom good news.
To others it is a judgment, a piece of bad news.
And it is good news because the reality of evil is trans-
    formed into a reality of goodness,
thanks to conversion.
Conversion implies overcoming the objective causes
    that generate sin,
produce injustices,
and distill death.

Without conversion the kingdom does not come,
nor does liberation take place.
Conversion calls for ruptures that will necessarily entail conflicts.

For the sake of liberation,
Jesus showed himself to be free
vis-à-vis religious traditions that were oppressing
    people,
contrary to God's will.
He confronted the pious people
who were using God as an alibi
for not seeing human beings and their needs
and for not heeding the demands of justice.
Jesus' God is the Father of infinite goodness
who treasures the poor,
the lost drachma,
the stray sheep,
and the prodigal son.
The worship that pleases God most
is service rendered to others,
and particularly to the lowliest ones
in whom God has hidden himself.
Jesus' prophetic criticism also attacks the powerful,
those who enjoy a monopoly
over possessions, knowledge, and power.
Jesus does not speak in terms of their interests,
but rather in terms of the interests and yearnings of the
    poor.
All this scandalized many,
and they got together
to get rid of Jesus.

Jesus was first condemned as one guilty of blasphemy.
The religious authorities realized that Jesus
identified himself with God.
Then Jesus was falsely condemned as a guerrilla-
    fighter before the political authorities.

Maligned, isolated, rejected,
threatened, and ultimately condemned to death,
Jesus did not strike a bargain in order to survive.
He remained loyal to God and to people of good will
even though that meant
he would be condemned to death.
He knew that his enemies were merely actors in a
    bigger drama,
whose chief protagonists were the Evil One
and the sin of the world.
In the last analysis it was this sinfulness,
which had taken root in human beings,
hardened their hearts,
and perverted fraternal relations,
that caused Jesus to be condemned to death.
Shouldering this condemnation in all his innocence,
Jesus freed us from sin.

It was the wicked . . .
who said among themselves,
thinking not aright: . . .
"Let us oppress the needy just man;
. . . let our strength be our norm of
    justice;
for weakness proves itself useless"
(Wisd. 1:15; 2:1,10,11).

Now:
Jesus continues to be condemned to death

The sinfulness of the world,
which killed the Son of God,
continues to kill the children of God.
Jesus' passion goes on
in the passion of our suffering people.
Everywhere we find a thirst for justice,
a hunger for equality,
and a yearning for brotherhood.
Efforts are being made to create the social, economic,
political, educational, and religious conditions
that will turn justice into a concrete reality
for the largest possible number of people.
Only when such conditions are created
will justice cease to be a mere desire.

Only then will it begin to be a concrete fact.
But it is at this point that the obstacles begin as well.

Those who live in a privileged situation
do not want to give up their privileges
so that others may have the things that they need
but that are now denied them.
Groups accustomed to the best
are not willing to give that up
and settle for what is merely good
so that other people in bad straits
might be able to live in a normal, decent way.
We see a criminal breach of fraternity
in family life, among social classes,
in the nation, and in international relations.

Some people are willing to serve as the sounding board
for the vast, powerless majority
and their cries for justice.
Some are courageous enough to be the voice
for those without voice or opportunity;
they join in solidarity with the latter's struggles,
sharing their outlook,
their language, their defeats,
their victories, and their destiny.
But it is mainly those treated unjustly themselves
who are taking their cause into their own hands,
uniting, organizing,
coordinating their ideas,
and arranging their practical deeds.
Without displaying a vengeful or oppressive spirit,
they are fighting to win their stolen dignity
and to recover their stolen rights.

The cause of the oppressed who are seeking justice
and reclaiming their rights
is the cause of God himself.
For God said:
"I have witnessed the affliction of my people . . .
and have heard their cry of complaint against their
    slave drivers,
so I know well what they are suffering.
Therefore I have come down to rescue them . . ."
    (Exod. 3:7–8).

In this truly messianic mission,
countless people are defamed, isolated,
persecuted, hurt in their work life and family life,
incarcerated, tortured,
exiled, and condemned to heavy assaults
because of their commitment to justice
and people's rights.
Wicked people with power will always say:
"Let our strength be our norm of justice" (Wisd. 2:11).

The condemnation of Jesus
is perpetuated in these people who fight for justice.
Jesus will continue to be condemned to death
so long as we do not establish the human and historical
    conditions
that will allow justice to flower
and right to flourish.
And without justice and right,
the kingdom of God will not be established.

SECOND STATION

Jesus
takes up
his cross

Jesus was led away,
and carrying the cross by himself,
went out to what is called the Place of
*   the Skull*
(in Hebrew, Golgotha) (John 19:17).

Then:
Jesus carried his cross

Once the sentence of condemnation was passed,
Jesus was handed over to the soldiers for torturing.
The Roman legionaries subjected poor people con-
    demned to death to terrible forms of torture.
The condemned were stripped, whipped,
and subjected to all sorts of indignities.
They were tossed from pillar to post like rubber balls
and made the butt of shameful derision.
God did not spare his Son.
He handed him over to these cruel barbarities
and allowed him to experience the depths of human
    wickedness.
Thus Jesus entered into solidarity
with all the downtrodden of history.

The Old Testament had already foretold the machina-
    tions of people against the just person:

"With revilement and torture let us put him to the test,
that we may have proof of his gentleness
and try his patience.
Let us condemn him to a shameful death;
for according to his own words,
God will take care of him" (Wisd. 2:19–20).
God did not protect Jesus,
nor excuse him from the obligation
to walk the narrow road of humiliation.
St. Peter offers this witness:
"When he was insulted,
he returned no insult.
When he was made to suffer,
he did not counter with threats.
Instead, he delivered himself up
to the One who judges justly" (1 Pet. 2:23).

The justice of God,
which will pass judgment on human justice,
will reveal itself with the brightness of sunshine
on the day of the Resurrection,
but not right now.
Now Jesus must drink the chalice of suffering down to
    the last drop.
He must walk the way of the cross to the very end,
enduring the limitless atrocities of injustice against the
    innocent.

The penalty of the cross was the most barbaric and
    terrible punishment of the ancient world.
It was inflicted on political rebels and slaves.
The Jews regarded it as God's curse.

After being tortured,
people condemned to crucifixion had to carry the in-
    strument of their own execution through the streets
until they reached the place of execution outside the
    city.
Jesus did just that,
until he reached the place of execution
outside the walls of Jerusalem.

But it was not only then
that Jesus began to carry his cross.
A cross is not just a piece of wood.
It is everything that makes life difficult:
the "crosses" we have to bear in life.
It is everything that causes us suffering,
particularly in our efforts to be just
and to create more fraternal social relationships.
That is carrying our cross day by day.
Jesus uncomplainingly carried the crosses of his life
as a poor person and an itinerant prophet.
He accepted not only the tormenting limitations of a
    spirit in the flesh
but also the contradictions of a God made flesh in a
    sinful world.
In a calm and courageous way
he put up with the machinations of the scribes,
the opposition of the Pharisees,
and the lack of understanding among his own disciples.
He endured the great temptation in the garden of
    Gethsemane with sweat and blood.
Now he does not simply accept the cross that is im-
    posed on him by the Jews and the Romans.

He embraces it freely out of love.
He transforms the cross
from a symbol of condemnation
into a sacrament of liberation.

If a man wishes to come after me,
he must deny his very self,
take up his cross,
and begin to follow in my footsteps
(Matt. 16:24).

Now:
Jesus continues to carry his cross

All liberation and all real growth in right and justice
  have their price.
The present condition of the world
and the ways in which it is organized today
contradict God's project in history.
God's aim is to establish his kingdom,
a kingdom in which all human beings
will be his children, free and obedient children,
and truly brothers and sisters to one another.
The kingdom of God in the world
is being built up in opposition to the rule of sinfulness,
  egotism, and poverty.
God does not want to see poverty
because it is the product of unjust social relationships.

God's kingdom divides.
Not every attitude or type of growth is acceptable to
  God.

There are people who are too deeply attached
to their quest for wealth and power
that leave others out in the cold.
They have no sense of social responsibility.
They do not place their power in the service of causes
that will do justice to all.
Instead they place it in the service of causes
that will advance the interests of a few.
Power is legitimate only when it protects justice.
Those with power can practice violence to defend
   themselves.
They fashion crosses for those who fight for a world
that is less divided between rich and poor.
On those crosses they crucify the prophets
who proclaim a greater justice,
the advocates of the cause of the poor,
and the poor themselves.
The rightness of the poor's cause is not acknowledged.
Their quest for humanization and fraternity
is maligned as subversive,
as an incentive to violence.
But all those who fight for the cause of the poor
make Jesus come alive today,
carrying his cross through the long byways of history.

This cross,
imposed on people already crucified
by the dehumanized life they are forced to live,
is a crime that will not escape the judgment of God.
Since God himself was crucified in Jesus Christ,
no cross imposed unjustly
is a matter of indifference to him.
He is in solidarity with all those who hang on crosses.

Their humiliation is his humiliation.
They do not carry their cross by themselves.
Jesus carries it with them and in them.

This cross, shattering as it may be,
is a thing of dignity
because it is the result of a commitment with dignity:
i.e., to live and fight so that there will be fewer and
    fewer unjust crosses for others.
For there is a cross that gives dignity to the person
    crucified on it:
the cross imposed on those who fight against the
    crosses laid upon the lacerated shoulders of our
    downtrodden, humiliated people.
That was the cross of Jesus Christ.
It was not the cross of a subversive (Luke 23:2),
of your typical revolutionary.
It was the cross of a prophet who identified himself
    with the cause of God,
and God's cause is embodied in the cause of the
    downtrodden of this world.

That cross certainly brings torment to the body.
But even more certainly,
it brings grandeur and exaltation to the person in-
    volved.
That person becomes a liberator,
even as Jesus Christ was.
No trace is left
in human or divine memory
of those who inflicted the cross on others.
Only those are remembered who carried a cross
for the sake of others.

Jesus falls the first time

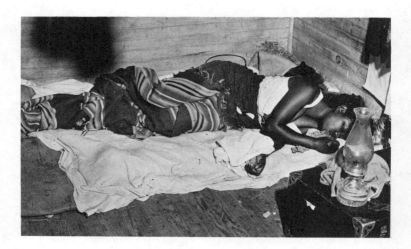

Jesus, . . .
carrying the cross by himself,
went out to what is called
the Place of the Skull (John 19:17).
He withdrew from them about a
*   stone's throw,*
then went down on his knees and
*   prayed (Luke 22:41).*

Then:
Jesus fell for the first time

Weakened by the loss of blood from torture,
suffering from hunger and thirst,
and bowed under the weight of the cross,
Jesus tottered and fell heavily to the ground.
How could the One
who keeps the whole universe on its feet
experience a fall?
And yet the eternal Son of God
did make firsthand contact
with the dust of the ground.

Falling is not just a physical accident.
Falling means recognizing freely and sincerely the
    limits of our strength

in the face of situations that are beyond us
and force us to submit.
Falling shows us our human frailty.
It reveals the fragile clay of which we are made,
showing us that we are neither omnipotent nor invul-
    nerable.
Confronted with such a fall,
we may nurture a spirit of revolt.
Refusing to accept our frailty,
we may raise our eyes,
if not an angry fist,
in a gesture of displeasure toward the calm sky.
Or we may nurture a spirit of resignation.
Compelled to recognize our limitations,
we may do nothing at all
to extricate ourselves from our plight.
There is a third possibility, however.
We can nurture the spirit of humility.
While calmly accepting our fall,
we may still trust in God,
whose strength comes to reinvigorate our weakness,
and get up again with renewed courage.

That is the humility that Jesus displayed in his life.
He was a fragile, poor person in this world.
Though he himself never sinned,
he assumed our full mortal condition,
stigmatized as it is by sin,
injustice,
and a breakdown in brotherhood.
As the Epistle to the Hebrews reminds us,
"he had to become like his brothers in every way"
    (Heb. 2:17),

and so "we do not have a high priest who is unable to
   sympathize with our weakness,
but one who was tempted in every way that we are,
yet never sinned" (Heb. 4:15).
Hunger, thirst,
fatigue, hot and cold weather,
an insecure life without a roof over his head,
tears, fear, sadness,
persecution, slander, death threats,
strong temptations, panic and anxiety over death,
imprisonment, torture, and crowning with thorns:
all these things were experienced personally
by the Son of Man when he walked among us.
"The Lord laid upon him the guilt of us all.
Though he was harshly treated,
he submitted and opened not his mouth.
Like a lamb led to the slaughter
or a sheep before the shearers,
he was silent and opened not his mouth.
Oppressed and condemned, he was taken away,
and who would have thought any more of his destiny?"
   (Isa. 53:6–8).

Being heroic does not mean staying on one's feet at all
   cost.
Being heroic means being willing to fall in solidarity
   with all those who pay the price for human frailty.
But being heroic also means getting up again after
   falling
and starting off again on the road chosen.
True grandeur means accepting our frailty without
   complaint,
remaining humble without showing resentment,

and confidently entrusting ourselves to our heavenly
   Father's arms.
Such is the grandeur shown to us by Christ
when he fell beneath his cross.

No pupil outranks his teacher,
no slave his master.
The pupil should be glad
to become like his teacher (Matt.
10:24–25).

Now:
Jesus is still falling

History is usually told by the victors.
It is they who preserve the written documents,
erect monuments,
and have epics sung about themselves
in order to immortalize their deeds.
Who will tell the history of the vanquished, the losers?
They are forgotten.
The devastation and suffering left behind
by those climbing to the top
are covered up.
The memory of such deeds is extinguished,
their guilt passed over in silence.
There is an anti-history of the fallen losers,
and only God knows the true dimensions of their
    bloody drama.
In every age "Rachel mourns her children,
she refuses to be consoled
because her children are no more" (Jer. 31:15).

There are the farmers who got together to defend their
    legal rights to their lands and were eliminated.
There are the Indian tribes who were driven off their
    reservations
and decimated by malnutrition and disease.
There are the factory workers who were fired, perse-
    cuted, and written off as people who had "disap-
    peared"
because they sought to make good their rightful claims
    to a just wage.

All these people fell.
They are Jesus falling again and again
in the course of history's Way of the Cross.
Jesus is already risen from the dead,
already in the glory of his Father.
But his resurrection is not yet complete
because his passion still goes on
in the passion of his brothers and sisters.

But these defeats are defeats only in the pages of the
    history we are living through.
They are not defeats in the eyes of God.
Job will always be heard by God,
who heeds the value of his sufferings.
God will not let the open wound go on bleeding indefi-
    nitely.
It is to such people that God promised the kingdom.
And it is all the more theirs
insofar as they do not succumb to feelings of impo-
    tence,
insofar as they work to anticipate it by enacting pro-
    found changes

that create the real preconditions for justice, peace, and
   reconciliation.

Hope exists for the sake of the hopeless.
If Christ continues to fall in history
in the falls of his brothers and sisters,
the reason is that falling renews our strength to keep
   getting up again.
All memory of suffering awakens dangerous visions,
visions that are dangerous for those who try to control
   the present or the future.
They are visions of the kingdom of justice,
which enable the suffering people to shake off their
   bonds
and to keep moving along the road to liberation.
All great and genuine revolutions
were made to do justice
to the suffering of the downtrodden in this world.

Human beings will never resign themselves
to staying flat on the ground.
They were made for the heights.
Like Jesus, they will always get up again,
pick up their crosses,
and keep on searching for a promised land of total
   liberation
for all those who are helping to free themselves
and their fellow human beings.

Since Christ got up from his first fall,
no fall need be fatal.
Humble remembrance of his fall
gives us reason for greater hope.

Jesus meets his afflicted mother

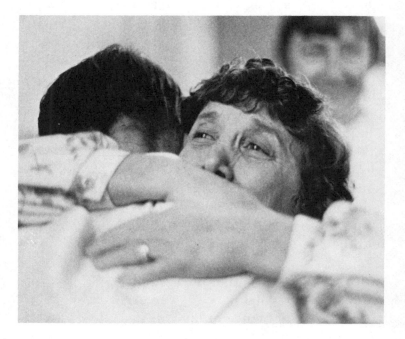

There were also women present. . . .
These women had followed Jesus
when he was in Galilee. . . .
Near the cross of Jesus
there stood his mother (Mark 15:40;
John 19:25).

Then:
Jesus met his mother

Still shaky from his fall,
his face covered with sweat and blood
and his eyes bulging,
Jesus happens upon the figure of his loving mother
in the midst of the noisy crowd.
The words stick in their throats;
they cannot even gesture to each other.
Only their glances meet.

Everyone is shouting, making accusations,
hurling insults, and harassing the condemned man.
Only Mary,
silent and powerless to help,
offers comfort and support
with her presence and her tears.

"Come, all you who pass by the way,
look and see whether there is any suffering like my
   suffering" (Lam. 1:12).
It is not enough that Jesus should suffer in body and
   soul.
Even our most sacred and intimate affection,
the affection we feel for our mother,
is crushed under his cross.
God demands everything from Jesus,
even his mother.
And Jesus surrenders her too.
He sees his mother humiliated and condemned too,
because every mother suffers doubly.
She suffers her own pain
and the pain of her child.

But "stern as death is love,
relentless as the nether world is devotion;
its flames are a blazing fire.
Deep waters cannot quench love,
nor floods sweep it away" (Song of Sol. 8:6–7).
Mary's love for Jesus is stronger than death.
The two of them are generating a redeemed life
that will no longer be menaced by death.

Right now, however, Mary must face the moment
   prophesied by old Simeon:
"You yourself shall be pierced by a sword" (Luke 2:35).
Mary has come to be with her son.
She shares the pain imposed on him unjustly.
She weeps the tears evoked by an unfair and wicked
   condemnation.

She freely shoulders it all with Jesus
in order to bring redemption, expiation, and liberation.
She is collaborating in the creation of a world
where no one will any longer have to be crucified;
at last the kingdom of God is beginning to take root.

The first to benefit in that kingdom
are the victims of injustice, oppression, and violence.
The powerful, the rich, and the proud
will be toppled from their places.
Thus they will be able to stop being inhuman.
Freed from the schemes that made them oppressors,
they too will have a chance to share in God's new order.
Even before the birth of Jesus,
Mary sang of the effects of this divine revolution in her
    hymn of praise,
the Magnificat.
She was courageous enough to raise her voice and say:
"He has shown might with his arm;
he has confused the proud in their inmost thoughts.
He has deposed the mighty from their thrones
and raised the lowly to high places.
The hungry he has given every good thing,
while the rich he has sent empty away" (Luke 1:51–53).

But this divine revolution and its hopes have a price.
Given the sinful condition of the world,
it will be effected only through the sacrifice of God's
    son, Jesus.
Out of love for human beings,
he freely accepts the crucifixion imposed on him by a
    judicial sentence.

In this way the kingdom,
which had been rejected,
is reintroduced into history.
With her tears, her sorrows, and her solidarity,
Mary,
the mother of Jesus,
helped to create the new state of the world,
a world finally liberated.

Remember that I stood before you
to speak in their behalf,
to turn away your wrath from them
(Jer. 18:20).

Today:
Jesus continues to meet Mary

Mary now lives with Jesus.
She was raised from the dead
and assumed into the glory of heaven.
And precisely because she is risen,
she lives within humanity in a mysterious but real way.
After Jesus,
no one is more closely united to all human beings
than Mary is.
Her assent to God's proposal to become a human being
associated her with all of human history.
The flesh through which God became our brother
was flesh received from Mary.
Even as Mary accompanied Jesus on his journey to
      Calvary,
so she now accompanies him on his journey
through the centuries until his glorious coming.

There is a feminine, maternal dimension
in the salvation that God has brought us.

That dimension comes from Mary
because she is the mother of Christ
and the mother of human beings.
God's salvation is tender,
like a mother's love.
It is warm and comforting,
as is a mother when she takes her baby in her arms,
caresses it, and feeds it (Jer. 11:1–4).
It is total and radical,
like the love of a wife and mother (Isa. 49:15–16).

Mary continues to feel compassion for her children.
She accompanies them in their sufferings.
She offers them strength and encouragement
with her look of understanding, support, and approval,
even as she did for Jesus.
Living in glory,
she is not indifferent to the human drama.
Even as in the Magnificat she took sides
with the lowly against the proud,
the poor against the powerful,
so now she continues to raise up courageous women
    committed to achieving justice
and to overcoming the age-old forms of discrimination
    against women.
As Paul VI put it,
Mary "does not disappoint any of the deeper aspira-
    tions of human beings today.
Indeed she offers them the perfect model of what a
    disciple of the Lord is:
a worker in the earthly, temporal city
and at the same time a wise pilgrim
on the way to the heavenly, eternal city;

a promoter of justice that liberates the oppressed,
and of charity that succors the needy;
but most of all, an active witness to love,
which builds up Christ in our hearts."

Even as she inspires forces seeking to transform the
    world into the kingdom of God,
so she shares in the sorrow that accompanies the life of
    human beings.
In those who are laden with life's burdens and crosses
she sees the figure of her own son, Jesus.
To all her human children she shows the same loving
    compassion
that she had for her son.
She is the Virgin of Sorrows
as well as the Virgin of Joys,
because she knows how to make our tribulations her
    own.

Accompanied by such a loving mother,
we find the strength to carry our cross
until we reach the point where suffering will end
and full liberation will break through.

Simon the Cyrenean helps Jesus to carry his cross

As they led him away,
they laid hold of one Simon the Cyre-
*   nean*
who was coming in from the fields.
They put a crossbeam on Simon's
*   shoulder*
for him to carry along behind Jesus
*   (Luke 23:26).*

Then:
Simon the Cyrenean helped Jesus

Jesus has nearly fainted.
His steps are uncertain,
but there is still a long way to go.
He might succumb to hemorrhaging
or to the heavy weight of the cross.
A fellow returning from the fields is grabbed by those
    in charge.
He is a strongly built farmer.
He is forced, against his will, to carry Jesus' cross.
Even though he was averse to the idea,
Simon performed an act of real solidarity.
He helped a condemned man in his weakened condi-
    tion.
History will gratefully preserve his memory and his
    name.

His sons, Alexander and Rufinus,
were known to the early Church.

Simon certainly had nothing to do with Jesus.
He did not know who he was,
much less that he himself was helping the Son of God
and the Liberator of the world.
But that does not matter.
What matters is that in a moment of need
Simon was capable of lending his shoulders
to one whose own had given out,
of offering his strength to one who had none left,
of taking on himself the cross
which the other man could no longer carry.

It is important to be familiar with, to take cognizance of,
people and situations.
It is important to know that Jesus is the Lord,
that he represents the personal and definitive visit of
   God to humanity.
It is important to realize that we must be sensitively
   aware of the urgent needs of others,
especially of those who are most poor, dirty, and foul-
   smelling.

But knowing is not the decisive thing.
The decisive thing is real, effective action.
It is not those who know and say "Lord, Lord" who will
   be saved
but rather those who do what God asks.
Salvation takes place
when we make the leap from theory
to real, authentic practice.

We attain salvation when we engage in real solidarity,
unselfish love, sincere pardoning,
and the offer of a generous helping hand.

Simon the Cyrenean was a good Samaritan to Jesus
as he suffered on his journey to Calvary.
The man he helped was not just a condemned criminal
     in the eyes of Jewish and Roman justice.
Simon helped God himself.
"Lord, when did we see you suffering
and help you?
When did we see you lying in a pool of blood
and pick you up?
When did we see you carrying your cross
and help you by shouldering it ourselves?"
And the Lord will say to us:
"I tell you truly,
every time that you act like Simon the Cyrenean,
who carried the cross of a condemned man,
you do it for me."

God really does lie hidden and unknown beneath
     every person in need.
God pleads for compassion and liberation.
God wants to be helped.
It is important to know this.
But even more important and decisive is offering help,
stooping down and taking the other person's cross on
     our shoulders,
and walking along together.
This is the perduring lesson that Simon the Cyrenean
     has left us.

This, rather, is the fasting that I wish:
releasing those bound unjustly,
untying the thongs of the yoke;
setting free the oppressed,
breaking every yoke (Isa. 58:6).

Now:
Simon the Cyrenean continues to offer help

In judging our salvation or definitive damnation,
God will not be guided by cultic criteria
—when and how we pray—
nor by doctrinal criteria
—what truths we believe in.
God will be guided by ethical criteria:
what we did for others.
The eternal destiny of human beings will be measured
by how much or how little solidarity we have displayed
with the hungry, the thirsty,
the naked, and the oppressed.
In the end we will be judged in terms of love.

And the poor and needy will judge us in the name of
   God:
"You saw me passing by hungry.

You saw my children eating from the garbage heap
and did not offer me the scraps from your full plate.
You saw me torn to shreds,
my family buried in a cruddy shack,
and yet you drove me away
and took my little patch of land to build your mansion.
You saw a whole class of people decimated by starva-
    tion wages and dehumanized by dire need,
and yet you showed no fellowship with them.
You denounced their leaders as subversives,
their ideas of justice as assaults on the security of the
    affluent in society,
and their organized activity as violent rebellion de-
    signed to destroy peace.
So, since you did not choose to live in fellowship,
you are condemned to live in eternal loneliness.
Since you were insensitive to justice,
you will not be able to live with the just.
You have already had your consolation in life!"

The poor are not just another theme in the Gospel.
They are of the very essence of the Gospel,
or evangel,
which means "good news."
It is the good news or joy of messianic justice
for those who have been treated unjustly,
of liberation for those who have been oppressed,
of salvation for those who find that they are lost.
Only from the standpoint of the poor
can we understand the hope embodied in the gospel
    message of Jesus.

And we can be saved only if we adopt the perspective
   of the poor.

The Gospel is certainly addressed to all.
All are challenged and summoned by it:
those who control the goods of this world
and those who do not;
those who are privileged to enjoy knowledge
and the ignorant.
The Gospel is not confined to one class.
But participation in the kingdom of God and salvation
   are only for those who,
even though they may be rich,
take upon themselves the cries of the poor and seek
   justice;
for those who inscribe in their own life's project the
   yearning of the poor
for an equitable, fraternal societal life
and who then help to turn this yearning into a reality.

In this world there will always be great, self-sacrificing
   spirits who,
though belonging to a more favorably placed social
   group,
will join in solidarity with those on the bottom,
embody their hopes,
and suffer their dire plight.
Like Simon the Cyrenean,
there will always be individuals and entire classes
who will help to carry the cross of Jesus
as he suffers and almost succumbs
in the lives of millions of laborers.

Veronica wipes the face of Jesus

A pious woman wiped Jesus' face.
(Tradition of the Jerusalem Church).

Then:
Veronica wiped the face of Jesus

Sweat and blood pour off the face of Jesus.
In the crowd of curious onlookers a woman,
Veronica,
is taking it all in.
At critical moments it is always the women who show
    the most courage.
Suddenly Veronica breaks through the barrier of sol-
    diers,
approaches Jesus,
and wipes his bloodied face.

Wondrous to behold,
his face is left imprinted on the towel.
It is a suffering face,
disfigured with wounds.
Yet this was the only image of himself that Jesus chose
    to bequeathe us.
He gave us,
not a healthy, handsome, perfect face,
but the face of the Suffering Servant
described many years before in the Book of Isaiah:

So marred was his look beyond that of man,
and his appearance beyond that of mortals. . . .
There was in him no stately bearing to make us look
   at him,
nor appearance that would attract us to him.
He was spurned and avoided by men,
a man of suffering,
accustomed to infirmity,
one of those from whom men hide their faces,
spurned,
and we held him in no esteem.
Yet it was our infirmities that he bore,
our sufferings that he endured,
while we thought of him as stricken,
as one smitten by God and afflicted.
But he was pierced for our offenses,
crushed for our sins;
upon him was the chastisement that makes us whole,
by his stripes we were healed (Isa. 52:14; 53:2–5).

Here is a lesson to be learned and lived.
Jesus wants to be recognized in the light of those
   humiliating signs.
Power, glory, and wealth can include God,
but they do not lead directly to God;
they do so only insofar as they are relativized and
   purified.
In becoming incarnate,
the eternal Son did not assume the symbols of power,
the trappings of glory,
or the ostentatious signs of wealth.

Instead he chose for himself
poverty, humility, and weakness.
Those signs lead directly to God
because they clothed the historical body of God's Son.

Jesus bequeathed us the image of his disfigured face
to give direction to our search for God.
The imprint on Veronica's towel is a signpost pointing
    the way.
God wishes to be encountered and served
in the face of this humiliated and outraged person,
in the disfigured face of this man who was the victim of
    violence.
It is easy to recognize the Lord's face
in the artistic works that are part of our faith's tradition.
It is even easier to encounter his visage
upon hearing his voice and his words in Sacred Scrip-
    ture.
But it is awfully difficult to recognize his visage
in the faces, bodies, and lives of human beings
—particularly those who are despised by most people
because they are ugly,
disfigured by pain,
and creased by the lines of poverty.
Veronica extends her towel and tells us:
"In this face so devoid of grace and beauty
God reveals his face.
It is a face with a different kind of grace and beauty,
one which turns the nonhuman into a real human be-
    ing,
the disfigured into the image and likeness of God."

So marred was his look beyond that of
man,
and his appearance beyond that of
mortals . . . (Isa. 52:14).

Now:
Veronica is still wiping Jesus' face

Pious human beings will always ask:
Where do we find God?
Religions mark out the main places and the privileged
    situations in which we encounter God:
e.g., prayer, the interior life,
a lifestyle of simplicity and asceticism,
and unselfish service to our fellow human beings.
Christians know that they encounter God in the
    Church,
in its sacraments, in the sacred words of Scripture,
and in fraternal, loving encounter with their neighbors.

The question is legitimate and the answers relevant.
But we learn from Jesus that the truly basic question is
    a different one:
i.e., Where does God himself want to be encountered
    by human beings?

God chose to concentrate his presence,
to privilege certain situations.
If we do not encounter him there,
where he chose to be,
then we simply do not encounter him at all
nor do we commune with the real God of Jesus Christ.
First of all,
God chose to be encountered in Jesus Christ.
In the world Jesus was a frail, powerless human being,
so much so that other human beings were scandalized
    by him.
Yet in Jesus we find ourselves confronted with the
    eternal Son of God,
with the divine nature itself,
in this case living in the limited and seemingly insig-
    nificant confines of humanity.
To reject Jesus is to reject God himself
in his closest proximity to humanity.

Second, we encounter God
in the lives and faces
of the humiliated and the downtrodden.
God chooses to be recognized and served in them.
It is in the face of the afflicted and the oppressed
that God chooses to make clear
what he himself signifies.
First of all, the downtrodden raise a protest:
this situation contradicts the will of God,
and it is unacceptable to any human being
who has preserved the least trace of humaneness.
The situation must be repaired, or overcome.

In addition, the despised and oppressed
are the bearers of a great hope,
which manifests itself as a demand of justice.
They expect from heaven and from earth,
from human beings and from God,
that they will be able to recover their trampled dignity.

God considered this hope and this demand of justice so
     ineradicable
that he identified himself with the oppressed.
In their faces we find the face of God.
If we want to serve the true God rather than some idol
—whether the idol be pleasure, wealth,
self-assertion, religion,
or even our own version of ethical purity—
then we must do as Veronica did.
We must break out of the circle of self-absorption
and pay heed to the bloodied face of our fellow human
     beings.
For they are the great sacrament of God,
the signs and instruments of authentic divine reality.
If we do not share life with the oppressed,
we do not share life with God.

Veronica's veil brings to our minds,
for centuries to come,
the face of the Son of Man as the Suffering Servant.
When we wipe the face of our fellow human beings
who are suffering life as a painful passion,
we are wiping the face of Jesus.
He continues to present his suffering countenance
to the loving compassion of human beings.

Jesus falls
the second time

Jesus fell several times on his journey.
(Tradition of the Jerusalem Church)

Then:
Jesus fell for the second time

Stretched to the breaking point by his awful scourging,
bowed under the weight of the cross,
and worn out interiorly by the abandonment of all his
   friends and disciples,
Jesus stumbles and falls again under his cross.

The psalmist had well expressed what Jesus was feeling now:
"But I am a worm, not a man;
the scorn of men,
despised by the people.
All who see me scoff at me;
they mock me with parted lips,
they wag their heads . . ." (Ps. 22:7–8).
Once again we see the physical weakness that is mor-
   ally humiliating
because it limits a person's will to endure everything
   and act heroically.

Jesus personally experienced this humiliation.
It is what overtakes us when we seek to do something
  grand and do not succeed.
Jesus joined in solidarity with all those who suffer
  frustration and defeat,
particularly with those who meet failure in fighting for
  a more decent and just world.
He chose to take his place
beside the fallen and the downtrodden,
whom few people are willing to help back on their feet.

One of the most characteristic traits of Jesus of
  Nazareth
was precisely this solidarity with the lowly,
this compassion for the weak.
In proclaiming what ought to be,
in announcing the will and truth of his Father,
Jesus was stubborn and intransigent.
But when he came face to face with concrete human
  beings,
with sinners who had fallen,
he always proved to be merciful and understanding.
He never quenched the smouldering wick.

Jesus always took the side of the weak
and of those who were criticized on the basis of the
  prevailing social or religious norms:
i.e., the Samaritan, who was to be avoided as a heretic;
the publican, who was collaborating with the forces of
  the Roman occupation;
the centurion, who embodied the imperial authority of
  Rome and its rulers;

the adulteress, who was supposed to be stoned to
    death;
the Syro-Phoenician woman, who was a pagan;
the man blind from birth, the paralytic,
and the woman suffering from a flow of blood, whose
    illnesses were a sign of their sinfulness;
and his apostles, who were not fasting as the disciples
    of John the Baptist did.

Jesus' attitude was to accept all these people,
to make them realize that they were not beyond God's
    salvation
because of who or what they were.
God is a Father of infinite goodness.
He "is good to the ungrateful and the wicked" (Luke
    6:35),
to those open to conversion.
After all, "people who are healthy do not need a doctor;
sick people do" (Mark 2:17).
The mission of the Son of God
is "to search out and save what was lost" (Luke 19:10).

Jesus did not fear the consequences of his solidarity
    with such people.
It particularly irritated the pious Pharisees.
They conspired with the Herodians,
who were anxious to maintain the existing socio-
    religious situation at all costs,
as to how to get rid of Jesus.
If Jesus falls, he does so only to get up again
and to intensify his ties of solidarity
with all those who fall in history.

Is it possible that he
who did not spare his own Son
but handed him over
for the sake of us all
will not grant us all things besides?
(Rom. 8:32)

Now:
Jesus keeps falling again and again

Christians do not believe that the creation of a completely just, reconciled world
is within the possibilities of history and human willing
  alone.
The various forms of oppression are not just external;
they are deeply rooted in the human heart.
All of us have personal experience of the fact
that we cannot succeed in liberating ourselves.
We need someone to free our captive liberty
so that it will then be able to carry out its work:
i.e., love and proper relationships with persons.

Experience also teaches us that the actual achievement
  of justice is meager and fragile,
though human life would be ignoble and impossible
if we did not keep trying to achieve it.

On the other hand justice alone is not enough to maintain peace.
There must also be a gratuitousness and a self-giving
that transcend the imperatives of duty.
We need love and a capacity for forgiveness
that go beyond the limits of justice.

But we are not so lost that we can do nothing ourselves,
that we can only hope in God
and look to God for everything.
All of us possess the capability of paying heed
to the claims of reality for just, honest, loving relationships.
But what we fashion here is always fragile
and capable of disintegrating.
Failure, resignation, disbelief, and despair
are also part of our fallen situation.

Many people have been so crushed by life,
so beaten down by cruel injustices,
that they can no longer believe in hope.
Others have been so deeply marked by disgrace,
and particularly by misfortunes due to human malev-
olence,
that they become sceptics;
they cannot accept the idea that history as a whole has
some real meaning.
Still others give up,
grow weary of sublimating and hoping,
and surrender to their basic impulses;
they head down the path to pleasure and self-
destruction.

There is a whole army of irretrievable people,
who are considered dead weight in history.

And yet they count in God's eyes.
Salvation exists precisely for them.
The gospel message as the good news of liberation
is addressed principally to them.
The privileged audience of Jesus was the poor and the
    lowly:
i.e., those who cannot defend themselves,
the desperate, the defeated,
the nonhumans of the human race.
God's saving strength
shows itself in weakness (2 Cor. 12:9).
"He chose the world's lowborn and despised,
those who count for nothing,
to reduce to nothing those who were something"
    (1 Cor. 1:28).
It is the wisdom of the cross that confounds human
    wisdom.

Jesus, who was spurned by human beings (Isa. 53:3),
finds embodiment in all these people.
In them he continues to fall today.
It is on the ground that Jesus meets them.
It is there that he chooses to save them.

Jesus speaks to the women of Jerusalem

A great crowd of people followed him,
including women who beat their
breasts
and lamented over him (Luke 23:27).

Then:
Women wept for Jesus

When Jesus gets up the second time,
inspired by even greater courage to carry his cross to
   the end,
he is rewarded in a sense.
Though still stunned,
he hears the voices of women expressing compassion
   for him
and weeping to see him in such a pitiable state.

Feeling compassion is one way of sharing in the tragic
   plight of another person.
Human beings never completely lose their capacity to
   feel in themselves
the sorrow or pain suffered by another person.
For that other person is not just "other";
he or she is a fellow human being,
a brother or sister.
A sorrow shared is a sorrow alleviated.

There are bonds of unity
between those who are suffering
that are often stronger than the bonds of friendship
or even love.
The hell of abandonment and loneliness
meets its limits and its match
in the reality of compassion.
The day that no one has compassion for anyone
will signal the end of all hope
and the victory of hell over humankind.
And so Jesus finds renewed strength in the compas-
    sionate tears of the women nearby.

But Jesus' state,
pitiable as it is,
is not the most pitiable one.
More pitiable still is the state of those responsible for
    Jesus' suffering,
those who contravened the justice of God
and condemned Jesus to death
according to the norms of justice imposed by those in
    power.
Everyone knows from experience
that the greatest and most thoroughgoing misery
    derives,
not from unhappiness,
but from injustice.
Everyone realizes that the person
who practices injustice
is in a worse plight than the person
who suffers injustice.

Thus the people who should be lamented in this case
are those who condemned Jesus:
the Pharisees,
the scribes,
the elders,
the members of the Sanhedrin,
and Pontius Pilate.
Their state is truly pitiable
because it is a fountainhead of injustice,
ill will,
and malevolent interests.
It has caused the judicial murder of Jesus.

Jesus understands this tragic situation.
Aware of his own innocence,
he exhorts the weeping women:
"Daughters of Jerusalem,
do not weep for me.
Weep for yourselves
and for your children" (Luke 23:28).
These tears over those
who condemned Jesus
cannot be tears of compassion.
They are tears of unconsolable sadness
over the hardness of heart
that continually gives rise to fresh crimes.
They are a cry to heaven,
pleading for mercy
and for that heavenly strength
that can induce conversion
and thus halt the spiral of violence.

The weeping of the daughters of Jerusalem
was heard by the heart of God.
Jesus redeemed all.
To all he offers the opportunity to live a liberated life,
which will not call for weeping or lamentation ever
   again.

For our sakes God made him
who did not know sin,
to be sin,
so that in him we might become the
very holiness of God (2 Cor. 5:21)

Now:
Women are still weeping for Jesus

Human wickedness can be very subtle.
It can mask itself so well
that it can use for its own purposes
even the most authentically Christian symbols and virtues.
Even people with the best intentions can be deluded
into thinking that they are serving God
when in fact their actions are an offense against, and a
denial of, God.

Jesus' contemporaries condemned him,
thinking they were doing God a favor.
They did not heed what they were doing,
and so they made the most criminal mistake in history.
They killed the author of life,
our liberator.

If we do not possess the spirit of discernment,
we are doomed to repeat the same tragedy throughout
    the course of history.

Thus we find groups of people,
particularly among the well-to-do classes of society,
who use the symbol of the cross
and the fact of Christ's redemptive death
to justify the necessity of suffering and death
and to silence the cries of the oppressed
against injustices and their humiliating sufferings.
Appeals to the cross and redemptive suffering of the
    Lord
are used to hide the iniquity of those
who impose the cross and death on others
by virtue of their own selfish interests and practices.
Thus some people kill in God's name
while others are killed for the sake of God
and God's justice.

The cross of Christ cannot be used
to legitimate social attitudes and relationships
that impose oppression and unjust suffering
on one's fellow human beings.
The glory of God
does not consist in people being crucified
day after day by others;
it consists in a life of happiness and kinship
shared by all people.
Jesus was condemned to death precisely because he,
in his life and his preaching,

denounced those sinful attitudes
in the name of God's will.

Some tears arise from a recognition of mistakes and
    errors,
but they do not go so far
as to pinpoint the things
that have caused tears
in the first place.
Thus we may weep for our fellow human beings
who are subjected to terrible loneliness
in the jungle regions
and enslaved to very poor paying jobs,
or for those who are robbed of their land.
We may pity and even courageously protest
the malnutrition to which young children are subjected
in the slums and backlands.
We may deplore the exploitation of day-laborers
in our big cities.
This attitude expresses solidarity,
but it does not get to the root of the problem:
i.e., the accumulation of goods and wealth
in the hands of the few,
while the many go away empty-handed.
This is a sin against God
and our fellow human being.
Those responsible for this situation
are not in the backwoods,
the farmlands, the slums,
or in a house alongside the factory.
They are living in the great metropolitan centers.

In their hands are the decisions
whose effects they cannot see
because they take place far away.
By the same token
these people are immersed in a global system
that forces them to adapt to mechanisms
that generate injustices.

This whole mechanism,
with its underlying ideas
and its historical representatives,
must be subjected to the lash
of prophetic denunciation.
Here Christian practice must intervene
to help transform human relationships,
to provide for greater and fairer participation
by the vast majority.
Here is the main area
where conversion should take place
as an anticipation
and concrete embodiment
of God's kingdom.

Jesus falls
the third time

Before reaching Calvary,
Jesus fell heavily a third time
(Tradition of the Jerusalem Church).

Then:
Jesus fell again

Not far from the end of his journey,
the totally exhausted Jesus
cannot manage to stay on his feet.
He falls under his cross
for the third time,
opening up his sores and wounds once again.
But Jesus does not complain,
because he sees his sorrowful journey
as an offering to God
and his fellow human beings.
He does not regard this evil crushing of his life
as the fatal end to a life that always sought justice
but succumbed to the violence of those opposed to him.
Instead he sees his death as a self-sacrifice
freely proffered out of love for his friends
and his enemies.

With this third fall, however,
Jesus feels more defeated than ever.

He had spent his whole life doing good.
He had proposed the reality of the kingdom of God
to all human beings of good will.
It would be a kingdom of justice,
kinship, forgiveness of sins, divine filiation,
and definitive victory over the factors
that never cease to generate violence
and barriers between human beings.
Jesus hoped for a positive response to his proposal,
but instead he found opposition
from habitual interests
and a close-minded human project.
He found no openness to any summons
to overall structural changes,
to the possibilities of a new heaven
and a new earth.
So now Jesus lies flat on the ground,
defeated
and barely able to stand up again.

Human beings want a different kind of kingdom:
a kingdom that will sacralize the existing authorities;
a kingdom that will re-affirm
the already established truth of religion,
with its proofs and its laws;
a kingdom that will merely purify
all that exists in the world,
thereby ensuring its continued existence.
The kingdom of God
represented by Jesus
is of a different sort.
It is a kingdom of reconciliation,

but not at the price of concealing the conflicts
that cause violence against the lowly.
It is a kingdom of peace,
but its peace is the fruit of justice and conversion.
The kingdom of God does not exempt people
from transforming their attitudes and convictions,
or altering existing social relationships
of domination and subordination
so that they become truly fraternal ones.

The message of Jesus brings division and conflict
because it entails conversion,
and conversion implies ruptures and divisions.
Not everything in this world
is worth caring about or saving.
Jesus was imprisoned,
tortured,
and condemned to death,
and now he lies stretched out on the ground,
because not everything was worthwhile in his eyes.
He lived for
his Truth,
his Justice,
and his God
in opposition to the truth, justice,
and god of the Pharisees.
He was eliminated in the name of official justice,
the justice of the Pharisees.

But God pointed up the falsity of that justice,
and the idolatrous nature of its worship.
God took Jesus' part and raised him up,

to ensure the triumph of just truth and true justice.
There are truths for which one must die
if one wants to remain faithful to God,
one's own conscience,
and one's fellow human beings.
Jesus accepted death
because he chose to be faithful
to the very end.
Though lying prone on the ground,
he is more firmly planted on his feet than ever.

> *For my iniquities have overwhelmed*
> *me;*
> *they are like a heavy burden,*
> *beyond my strength (Ps. 38:5).*

Now:
Jesus will keep falling again and again

There is a type of suffering
that is the price one must pay
for living a virtuous life.
This suffering is meaningful
because it does good.
There is another type of suffering
that is inflicted on other people
by wicked human beings.
Causing suffering to others is an injustice,
and it indicts those responsible for it.
But when such suffering is patiently endured
as a sacrificial offering,
as it was in Jesus' case,
it is a way to personal redemption and merits,
with God's help,
the conversion of those who are causing it.
Finally, there is another type of suffering
that is the fruit of the sinfulness in the hearts of sinners.

It is good for nothing.
It is sadness in the worldly sense,
embodying condemnation.

The real "fall" of human beings
does not lie in their creaturely mortality or fragility;
it lies in their sinfulness.
Through our sinfulness
we transform ourselves from human beings
into non-humans,
from children of God
into rebels against God.

How does God react to sinners?
God obviously abominates sin,
because it is a rejection of love.
But God continues to love sinners
and to seek them out in their own peculiar cir-
    cumstances.
The God of Jesus Christ
loves the ungrateful and the wicked (Luke 5:36).
God lets the rain fall on both the just and the unjust.
God is profoundly merciful (Matt. 5:45),
ever ready to offer pardon
when we abandon our sinful course.

God does not make light of sin,
but takes it with absolute seriousness.
The cross shows how seriously God takes sin.
It is not a symbol of God's weakness.
It does not mean that God has given up the idea
of establishing right and justice on earth.

On the contrary, the cross expresses the power of God,
who is capable of transforming the sin
embodied in the cross
into redemption through the cross:
"And I
—once I am lifted up from earth—
will draw all men to myself" (John 12:32).

But God's offer of pardon takes effect
only when human beings give up their state of enmity
     toward God
and open up to divine mercy.
Otherwise they simply fashion their own damnation,
condemning themselves.
God does not hang back as a mere spectator
when power is utilized to oppress the weak
and crush the poor.
God does not keep sovereign distance
in the face of human crimes.
God's angry voice echoes through the centuries:
"Cain, where is your brother?"
God is mercy and pardon,
but does not exempt people from conversion.
Without conversion there is no justice,
no love,
nor even dialogue.

Many people live removed from God by their sins.
They suffer because they would like to live
in the proximity of grace
but cannot make it.
They fall again and again.

Some sinful mechanism traps them,
luring them into committing a sin they abominate.
They would undergo conversion
if they had the strength and the conditions of freedom.
Such people are not far from God.
Humble acknowledgment of their fallen situation
can drive them into the merciful arms
of their heavenly Father.
They are flat on the ground,
but their hope has not been suffocated to death.
Falling for the third time,
Jesus shoulders the tragic fall of such sinners.
By standing up again and recommencing his journey,
he saves them.

Jesus
is stripped
of his garments

When they had crucified him,
they divided his clothes among them
by casting lots (Matt. 27:35).

Then:
Jesus was stripped of his garments

F inally Jesus arrives at Calvary.
There is the altar of sacrifice
and the victim is readied.
The soldiers grab Jesus
and roughly strip off his clothes,
which are almost glued to the wounds
that cover his body.

It is a moment of utter shame.
Jesus finds himself naked and defenseless.
Clothes do not just cover the body.
They also conceal the personal mystery
that each human being bears within.
Human beings are naked
only when they are sharing with each other
the sacred mystery of their selves;
and of course we all stand naked before the living God,
to whom nothing is hidden or mysterious.
But Jesus is stripped naked
in front of an irreverent mob.

He is turned from an absolute subject
into an object of derision.
The outrage is not just against his body.
It is against that innermost core of the human person
inhabited by a sense of sacredness
and inviolable respect.

Jesus must sacrifice everything.
He holds nothing of himself back.
Here, on the threshold of death,
even more intensely than during his lifetime
he is a being-for-others.
He surrenders everything,
even the most intimate and private recesses
of his being,
in order to ransom all.

His garments are not handed over
to his closest relatives
as a final embodiment of tender, human ties.
They are divided up into four parts among the soldiers.
His seamless tunic, woven in one piece,
perhaps by the loving hands of his mother,
is raffled off in a dice game (John 19:24).
Then the soldiers offer him wine mixed with gall,
but Jesus refused to drink it
after he has tasted it (Matt. 27:34).
It was a potion designed to deaden the pains
of crucifixion.
Jesus preferred to experience the shattering power of
    suffering in all its forms
so that those who would come after him
might never feel alone in their sufferings.

Being stripped of his clothes
must have meant a new temptation for Jesus.
Stripped naked, many people feel totally defenseless.
All inner support falls away.
In such a situation they give up, turn back,
and betray the ideal for which they had previously
    endured torture and humiliation.

That is the helplessness of human fragility,
and Jesus shared it.
But he resisted the temptation with deep courage.
His suffering has dignity
because it is offered up lovingly for others.
He cannot renounce his decision to go all the way
because the sacrifice of his life
is the only way to establish close ties and reconciliation
with those who rejected him.

Stripping need not be simply an outrage.
Freely accepted by the innocent and the blameless,
it can be an opportunity for reconciliation
with their enemies.
They can be pardoned and enfolded
in the embrace of a truly universal love.

What you have done
is put aside your old self
with its past deeds (Col. 3:9).

Now:
Jesus is still being stripped naked

People have figured out every imaginable way
to make others suffer,
to destroy the human personality
with physical and psychological torture.
Yet people have also demonstrated an unbelievable
    capacity
for resisting and winning out over such torture
through the exercise of their freedom.
Even in defeat they can give meaning to their lives.
Rather than allowing themselves
to be conquered by evil,
they can overcome it with goodness.
They can offer up their lives as a sacrifice to God,
as a pardon for their enemies.
To those inflicting terrible tortures on them,
the martyrs can say:
"These are not tortures
but anointings for the sake of our Lord Jesus Christ.
On the road to liberation
death is the most sublime feast."

In such outrages
it is Jesus Christ who is being outraged,
for he suffers along with humankind
until the end of time.

Nothing makes people suffer more
than outrages committed against their moral dignity.
When they are subjected to physical and moral coer-
    cion,
they are forced against their will
to endorse what is false as true,
what is not fact as fact.
In such circumstances they feel really crushed.
It is not just that they are stripped of their clothes
and left naked and defenseless.
They also find themselves stripped of their spiritual
    garments,
of the courage that would allow them to endure to the
    end
and choose the glory of a violent death
over the joy of an accursed freedom.
After being subjected to the demolishing onslaughts of
    terror,
many find that they have been intimidated and deper-
    sonalized,
that they are an easy prey for manipulation by others.
They are victims of violence,
and such violence is a sin that cries out to heaven.
The sins that they may commit in such circumstances
and the blasphemies that they may utter with their lips
are, in God's ears, bitter prayers pleading for justice.
The Lord, who walked through that human hell,
will enfold them in his saving courage.

How many people have been stripped naked
in the subterranean depths of repressive systems and
　　mechanisms!
How many have been violated, bestialized,
and subjected to every kind of harrassment!
Husbands are forced to watch their wives being raped.
Wives are forced to see their husbands tortured and
　　castrated,
their daughters violated,
and their children executed.
These violations of the sacred rights of the human per-
　　son,
of the poor in particular,
are justified in the name of the legitimate defense and
　　security of society.
In fact, the security in question is only that
of society's privileged few.

In those outraged human beings
Jesus continues his Way of the Cross.
He continues to be stripped and humiliated
in his brothers and sisters.
With them he prays to his Father
that the kingdom may come,
a kingdom where weeping and death will be no more.

Jesus
is nailed
to the cross

> *With him they crucified two insur-*
> *gents,*
> *one at his right and one at his left*
> *(Mark 15:27).*

Then:
Jesus was crucified

Naked, Jesus is stretched out on the cross
while it is still lying on the ground.
Huge nails are hammered in
through his wrists
and through his feet.
Two Zealots, guerrilla fighters,
are crucified alongside him,
one on his right and one on his left.
Then the crosses are raised up
and firmly planted in the ground.
The condemned men could hang there for days.
Their piercing cries can be heard as far away as the city.
Jesus hears insulting remarks,
but he pardons the speakers:
"Father, forgive them,
for they do not know what they are doing."
He heeds the plea for the good insurgent:
"This day you will be with me in paradise!"

Concerned for his mother,
he entrusts her to John, his beloved disciple:
"Behold your mother!"

Through his life and message, Jesus,
acting in the name of God,
strove to inculcate in human beings a spirit
that would never cause crosses for others;
and now he himself hangs on a cross.
His cross is not the result
of an arbitrary whim on God's part.
It results from the way in which the world is organized.
Sinfully closed in upon itself,
the world rejected the God of Jesus
and eliminated Jesus himself.
The execution of Jesus
is the greatest sin ever committed
because it stands in opposition to God's will,
which is to establish the Kingdom
in the midst of creation.

God does not will death
but life in all its fullness.
That is another name for God's Kingdom.
Even though human beings rejected that Kingdom
and crucified Jesus,
who proclaimed and embodied it,
God did not cease to will it.
God found other ways to flesh it out in reality.
God's Son was required to remain faithful
to the divine plan
and to accept death as a consequence of his fidelity.

Jesus does remain faithful to the very end.
He does not fear conflict, insults,
imprisonment, and condemnation.
He is not afraid to die,
and he does not let fear of death stop him.
He goes on living and acting
in spite of the threat of death.
Not fear of death
but loyal commitment to the will of his Father
is the driving force of his life.
Though he knows he is going to die,
since all the factions are organizing to eliminate him,
Jesus still bears witness to his fidelity:
"I lay down my life to take it up again.
No one takes it from me;
I lay it down freely" (John 10:17–18).

Given the situation created by people's refusal
to undergo conversion,
Jesus really "had to die,"
as the Scriptures put it.
Now, nailed to the cross,
he knows for sure that he is going to die.
He does die,
out of fidelity to God and the plan for the Kingdom,
and out of fidelity to human hopes for a world
that will offer happiness and justice to all.

It is now through the death of his Son
that God will realize the Kingdom.
Jesus freely accepted condemnation to death.
He died for our sins.

In other words,
he died because our rejection of conversion
brought on his death.
He took our sins upon himself,
establishing solidarity with sinners
in order to free them from their wickedness.
In particular, he established solidarity with all the vic-
    tims of human sinfulness.
Nailed to the cross,
Jesus expresses his freedom to the fullest,
surrendering himself to God and human beings
out of love.

Christ loved you.
He gave himself for us
as an offering to God.
We are . . . heirs with Christ,
if only we suffer with him
so as to be glorified with him
(Eph. 5:2; Rom. 8:17).

Now:
Jesus continues to be nailed to the cross

There is a mysterious presence of God within humanity.
The Incarnation means that the Son
really did assume our sinful condition.
Once he did that, he continues to remain in it forever.
He became incarnate,
not to sacralize the world and humanity,
but to liberate them,
to make the old world new
and the sinful human being just.
His struggle to achieve this liberation
goes on through the centuries,
confronting all the obstacles
that the hardness of the human heart
and the iniquity of socio-historical relationships can
create.

Such conflict and confrontation is inevitable
because there can be no reconciliation
between God's project of liberation
and sin's project of domination.
The shift from the latter to the former
takes place through conversion.

Persecution and physical elimination
of the witnesses to the Kingdom
will not succeed in stopping the process
leading to the establishment of a new heaven
and a new earth.
This process is the cause of God.
And if God is for us,
who can be against us?
Even opposition and apparent defeat
nurture and accelerate the advent
of God's definitive Kingdom.
Yet, despite certainty of victory,
we continue to tread a universal Way of the Cross.
The cost of a happy outcome
is being paid from generation to generation.
The passion goes on.
Definitive resurrection will come
only at the end of the world.

So Jesus continues to be crucified
in all those who are crucified in history.
He is crucified in the millions who go hungry every day
and in those who are subjected to inhuman working
    conditions.
He is crucified in all those who are mutilated in war
and confined to hospital beds.

He is crucified in those who are marginalized
in our cities and rural areas,
and in those who suffer from discrimination
because of their race, sex, or poverty.
He is crucified in those who are persecuted
because of their thirst for justice,
and in those who are forced in their jobs
to violate their conscience,
to conceal the truth,
and to act as agents for institutions that oppress the
     lowly.
He is crucified in all those who fight,
without immediate success,
against economic and ideological systems
that generate sinful structures,
structures engaging in exploitation.
He is crucified in all those who are forced
to live within such structures against their will.

There are not enough Stations of the Cross
to depict all the ways in which the Lord continues to be
persecuted,
imprisoned,
condemned to death,
and crucified today
in the ongoing Passion of human life.

But Jesus does not just suffer.
He continues to offer himself to God
and his brothers and sisters,
to pardon,
and to love all human beings
to the very end.

Jesus dies on the cross

"My God, my God,
why have you forsaken me?"
Then Jesus, uttering a loud cry,
breathed his last (Mark 15:34, 37).

Then:
Jesus died abandoned on the cross

Jesus was expelled from the solid ground of earth.
Raised up on a cross,
he hung between heaven and earth
for three agonizing hours.
Human refusal could decree Jesus' crucifixion,
but it could not define the meaning
that the crucified Jesus would give to his crucifixion.
He would define it as love,
self-sacrificing love
designed to win pardon for those who crucified him
and for all human beings.
He would define it as solidarity
with all those crucified in history
as victims of human hardness of heart,
rigidified social structures,
and human rejection of the reality of God's Kingdom.

Yet, despite his limitless love for others,
Jesus would face one final, terrible temptation.

Designed to sully his love,
it would only help to bring it out more clearly.
Jesus' agonizing struggle now is with his Father.
The Father
whom he felt so intimately attached to as Son,
the Father
whom he had proclaimed to be so merciful and good,
the Father
whose Kingdom he had proclaimed and anticipated in
    his liberating praxis—
that same Father
now seems to have abandoned him completely.
Jesus suffers the hell of God's absence.

Around three o'clock in the afternoon,
minutes before the final denouement,
Jesus cries out in a loud voice:
"Eloi, Eloi, lama sabachthani?...
My God, my God, why have you forsaken me?"
Jesus is on the verge of despair.
From the innermost depths of his soul
well up questions
that attest to his worst temptation:
Is my fidelity to be absurd and meaningless?
Was there no sense to my struggle with the Pharisees
    for God's sake?
Was it in vain that I faced up to risk,
persecution,
legal condemnation,
and capital punishment?

Jesus finds himself naked, impotent,
and totally empty before his Father,

who now reveals himself in all his mysteriousness.
There is nothing for Jesus to lay hold of.
By human standards he has failed completely.
Even his own inner certainty has wilted away.
But even though the ground has given way beneath his
    feet,
Jesus continues to trust in his Father.
He cries out to him,
surrendering himself to the Mystery
that ever remains nameless.
That Mystery is Jesus' only hope and security,
his only support.

Jesus' absolute hope is understandable
only in the light of his absolute despair.
Where despair abounded,
there hope superabounded.
The grandeur of Jesus lies in the fact that he confronted
    and overcame this terrible temptation.
It prompted him to abandon all self-centeredness,
to surrender himself totally to God.
Thus his death would be complete,
his sacrifice perfect.
Jesus' last words embody his full self-surrender,
offered in freedom rather than in fatalistic resignation:
"Father, into your hands I commend my spirit. . . .
Now it is finished" (Luke 23:46; John 19:30).

You can depend on this:
If we have died with him,
we shall also live with him
(2 Tim. 2:11).

Now:
Jesus is still dying on the cross

Those who commit themselves
to the following of Christ
pledge to share his life and destiny.
Like Jesus,
they do not regard life
as something to be enjoyed egotistically
but rather as service
to their fellow human beings,
particularly to the neediest.
Such service may even entail
the sacrifice of one's own life,
offered as an expression of love and personal freedom.
If one's life is to be truly redemptive,
God often strips a person of everything.
Deprived of all consolation, certainty, and security,
the person becomes like Jesus
in his abandonment on the cross.

The history of human struggle
for justice and freedom
knows few successes.
It is full of martyrs,
defeats,
and long-standing hopes.
It is a history of unrestrained, inexhaustible hope.
The oppressors almost always win the day.
God has guaranteed final victory
in the triumph of the Kingdom of love and goodness,
but God allows the Way of the Cross,
with its suffering and seeming failure,
to go on from one century to the next.

Thousands of innocent people die every year,
victims of the hatred that they sought to overcome.
Thousands are abandoned to their fate every year,
often left without support by their brothers and sisters
who share the very same faith.
Thousands suffer desperation and agony,
unable to see the fruitful triumph of the cause
for which they are sacrificing themselves.
Committed by their faith to help create a world more in
    conformity with God's plan,
they do not get to see the results.
As Sacred Scripture describes their plight:

  Still others endured mockery, scourging,
  even chains and imprisonment.
  They were stoned, sawed in two,
  put to death at sword's point;

they went about garbed in the skins of sheep or goats,
needy, afflicted, tormented.
The world was not worthy of them.
They wandered about in deserts and on mountains,
they dwelt in caves and in holes of the earth.
Yet despite the fact that all of these were approved
     because of their faith,
they did not obtain what had been promised
                                    (Heb. 11:36–39).

There are countless prophets of sacred causes
that espouse the rights of the poor.
Some are known;
the vast majority are anonymous.
They all share the impotence and helplessness
of Jesus on the cross.
They are asked to accept the most difficult assignment:
to hope against hope,
to love what does not seem to be present to them,
and to believe in what they cannot see.
They are asked to endure the worst plight a human
     being can experience:
to die feeling abandoned by the God
for whom they lived and sacrificed their lives.

Still, they do not abandon God.
They surrender themselves to God in complete confi-
     dence.
In total inner emptiness
they cling to the nameless Mystery
that is infinitely beyond them.

For this mysterious God holds the secret meaning
of all their failed quests,
of all the absurdities of history.
To die like that is to share Jesus' death on the cross.
It is to share his redeeming mystery,
which will go on through history
until the world reaches its end and fulfillment
in the liberation of the last sinner
who opens to God's mercifulness.

Jesus
is taken down
from the cross

Near the cross of Jesus
there stood his mother,
his mother's sister,
Mary the wife of Clopas,
and Mary Magdalene (John 19:25).

Then:
Mary wept over her son

Jesus hangs lifeless on the cross.
A soldier comes along and pierces his side and his heart
    with a lance.
Two disciples whose love won out over their fear,
Joseph of Arimathea and Nicodemus,
take his body down from the cross.
They anoint it and wrap it in cloth with perfumed oils.

Now Mary takes the broken body of her son in her arms.
The singular serenity of his pale countenance transfi-
    gures his wounds.
His stigmatized body recovers a rare beauty.
While Mary caresses his body and weeps,
she may well have spoken such words as these:

My son, my son,
what have they done to you?

You proclaimed a great liberation to them,
and look at the disastrous failure they have imposed
  on you!
You healed so many people with those hands,
and look how they have pierced them with nails!

My son, my son,
what have they done to you?
You restored life to so many people,
and look how many conspired to take your life away
  from you!
You did only good,
and look at the evil they did to you!

My son, my son,
what have they done to you?
What more should you have done that you did not
  do?
Did you not give them their bodies,
their clothes, and their lives?
And yet they hung you up on a cross!
What more should you have done that you did not
  do?
Did you not give them all their blood?
And yet they pierced your heart!

Ah, my son,
you did the will of your Father,
who wanted you to be faithful to the very end.
You chose not to accommodate yourself to this world.
You wanted to see the full consummation,
the Kingdom of your Father with its justice and
  brotherhood.

Rest, my Son.
Through your life, self-sacrifice, and death,
your Father takes pity on the world
and offers it salvation.

Lying on the ground,
the lifeless body of our Lord poses an inescapable
    question:
Who will pay for suffering that is inflicted on people
    unjustly?
God is not heedless of crimes, sins, and their victims.
"This generation will have to account for the blood of
    all the prophets shed since the foundation of the
    world" (Luke 11:50),
and for the blood of the supreme prophet, Jesus.

God demands reparation for injustice,
and this reparation takes the form of conversion.
The cry against injustice will not be stilled
until justice prevails.
Even in death Jesus continues to stand
for the establishment of the reign of justice
and the homeland of love.
In death he embodies the most radical poverty
and the most complete self-emptying.
It is the precondition required if one is to be com-
    pletely God's
and to be filled with God's richness.
If the seed does not die,
it will not live!

Even now I find my joy
in the suffering I endure for you.
In my own flesh
I fill up what is lacking
in the sufferings of Christ (Col. 1:24).

Now:
Mary continues to weep over her children

Everything grows quiet in the face of death.
Fighting and conflict cease.
A corpse, even when it is mangled and rejected,
imposes holy respect and reverent silence.
We are confronted with a mystery.
It is not within the power of human beings
to decide about the ultimate meaning of life.
That is up to the One who holds the key to all secrets
and the answer to all questions,
who knows where every course will lead.

When we confront the inert corpses
of those who have fallen in the fight for a just cause,
we feel driven toward Someone greater
who will not allow the triumph of absurdity.
There must be some ultimate meaningfulness,
some definitive, certain sense,
for those who died on behalf of others;

for those who chose the most difficult path for themselves
because they loved the poor
and sought justice for them;
for those who preferred a violent death
to a life without dignity.

Every death leaves behind an open question.
We wait and look for the glimmer of some light
that will dispel all the shadows surrounding the mystery of life.
Death should not be the last word on life,
nor despair the final state of human beings.

History does not cherish the memory of those who
   killed.
Rather than holding despots up as an example,
it exalts the courage of those who endured death,
who shouldered the sufferings of the lowly,
and who undertook liberating revolutions.

Taken down lifeless from the cross,
Jesus paves the way for others
to pick up his banner and carry it forward.
They are the people who have come to understand
what God's project is:
the establishment of a world
where all will finally be brothers and sisters,
and children of the same Father,
in justice, liberty, and love.

There will always be human spirits
who will not resign themselves to cynicism,

self-indulgence, and pragmatism;
who will not join the ranks of those
who trust only in the order and power of the strongest.
Like Jesus, they will dream of a just world for all
and accept the risks entailed in establishing it.
And they will continue to be condemned
and crucified
for this hope of theirs.
But their ideas will not be buried with their corpses.
Instead their dead bodies,
lacerated by injustice,
will become the seed-bed of new followers.

Christ's passion is being completed
by each succeeding generation and its martyrs.
Their blood will keep crying out to heaven
for the advent of God's Kingdom.
Mary weeps for them,
even as she wept for Jesus.
And God will heed the supplication
of his Son's mother.

All these dead are to be found in the dead Jesus.
The question of all of them rises as a cry to God:
How long, O Lord, how long?
And the Lord,
who is merciful,
resurrects our hope,
transforming the question into a plea:
Thy Kingdom come . . .
on earth as it is in heaven!

Jesus
is placed
in the tomb

Then, having bought a linen shroud,
Joseph took him down,
wrapped him in the linen,
and laid him in a tomb
which had been cut out of rock.
Finally he rolled a stone across the
*   entrance of the tomb (Mark 15:46).*

Then:
Jesus was buried

After washing and anointing the body of Jesus,
Joseph of Arimathea wrapped it in a linen sheet
and laid it in his new tomb hewn out of rock (Matt.
    27:59–60).
In death, as in life,
the Son of Man had no place of his own to lay his head
    (Luke 9:58).
His body is dead,
but his life is hidden in God.
He will spend three days and three nights
in the bowels of the earth (Matt. 12:40).
We join with the Church in believing in Jesus Christ,
who "suffered under Pontius Pilate,
was crucified, died, and was buried . . .
descended into hell. . . ."

To "descend into hell" means to really die,
to experience the ultimate loneliness
where we have our decisive encounter with God.
By dying Jesus shared the loneliness of death,
the feeling of leaving behind this world,
this life, this earthly body, other human beings,
and all words of love and consolation.

We all fear death
because we seek to flee from the void of nothingness.
By his death Jesus
descended to the ultimate depths of aloneness.
He descended there so that he could offer us words of
     assurance:
"Do not be afraid.
I hold the keys of death.
I have overcome death
and pierced the depths of the ultimate loneliness.
I am there
where there once was nothing present.
Where ultimate abandonment once dwelled,
there my warmth now dwells.
Where death once reigned,
there now dwells life."

Jesus' solidarity with us,
reaching to the most hellish depths of our life,
liberated us once and for all.
All who die,
die with Christ.
We will never again die alone.

For Jesus,
to descend into hell
also means to redeem and liberate
all human beings in the world.
No one is beyond the reach of his redeeming action,
neither those who lived before him
nor those who will come after him.
The human beings who lived before Jesus
are removed from Jesus only by the calendar,
by chronological dating.
They are not remote from him
insofar as faith, hope, and love are concerned.
All who lived by these virtues will encounter Jesus.
Thanks to God's will,
all are umbilically united with Christ.

Finally, to descend into hell
means to descend into the very heart and soul of the
    earth (Matt. 12:40).
Death does not really mean
abandoning the world and life.
Rather, it means that human beings penetrate
the very heart and soul of matter.
Through death we leave a part of the world,
our body,
to assume the world in its totality.
Death is far more a gain than a loss.
In his death and burial Christ penetrated the very bow-
    els of the earth (Matt. 12:40).
As God incarnate he had already done that.
Now this truth acquires a cosmic dimension.

God incarnate,
Jesus Christ,
is inside our world.
He is opening up the cosmos to God
and making it the vehicle of God's presence.

Jesus buried inside a rock
symbolizes and makes concrete
the new situation of the world.
Thanks to his redemptive work,
the world is now the tabernacle of God.

Unless the grain of wheat
falls to the earth and dies,
it remains just a grain of wheat.
But if it dies,
it produces much fruit (John 12:24).

Now:
Jesus is still being buried

The meaning of death is defined
by the meaning of life.
Living is a great deal more than simply not dying.
It is carrying out a mission,
committing oneself to fashion some meaning
that will attain eternity.
Time does not create enough space
for us to completely realize the meaning of life.
Our desires, our hopes, our love,
our capacity to communicate,
and our powers of understanding
surpass and transcend everything that might present
    itself to us.
In wanting the world,
human beings seek the Absolute that is God
and that surpasses the limits of this world.

Death brings the end of this life.
It breaks our ties with the world,
with those we love,
and with our own bodily life.
But because human beings
are greater than the world,
they also prove to be stronger than death.
Death is the necessary step to fullness of life.
Through death life reaches its true end:
i.e., total self-fulfillment
in the full realization of all its potential.
With the death of the body,
all the barriers imposed by space and time,
by matter and corporeality,
collapse.
The human being within,
whose desire is insatiable,
whose love is limitless,
whose intelligence is unfathomable,
can now reach its full flowering.
Human desire is satiated,
human love finds its true object,
and human intelligence becomes a transparent vision
   of all things.
Thus death proves to be the true birth of the human
   being.
It is not an end to be lamented,
but a goal to be aspired to.

By the same token, however,
death finds its meaningfulness in life.

Life goes beyond death
because life is called to life,
not death.
That is the plan of its Creator.
But life blossoms into full flower
only in those who nurture life
here on this earth;
in those who defend its rights,
protect its dignity,
and are even willing to accept death
in their witness to it.
Those who violated life,
deprived others of life,
and crucified the living
will ever remain seeds that failed to take root,
buds that failed to open,
and cocoons that were forever closed in upon them-
    selves.
Their fate is absolute and total frustration.

All those who died like Jesus,
sacrificing their lives out of love
for the sake of a more dignified human life,
will inherit life in all its fullness.
They are like grains of wheat,
dying to produce life,
being buried in the ground
only to break through and grow.
It is thanks to them
that history goes on as a pageant of hope,
and that the Kingdom of God gains credibility.

The fullness of life implies resurrection.
The lifeless corpse is like an empty chalice
ready and able to take in the precious wine.
The resurrection will give the full measure of divine
    life to the body,
transfiguring human life.
It will make our life infinite, divine, and immortal.

Jesus
is raised up to life
in all its fullness

Why do you search for the Living One
among the dead?
He is not here;
he has been raised up (Luke 24:5–6).

Then:
Jesus' resurrection is the triumph of justice

Three days after his death
Jesus emerged alive
into the fullness of human and divine life.
Now everything became clear:
the meaning of our hope,
the nature of true justice,
and the side that God is on.

The resurrection is the plain and simple concretization
of the Kingdom of God,
which is a kingdom of life, justice, and goodness.
God did not abandon Jesus.
In the resurrection God proves
that he is completely on Jesus' side.
The resurrection represents a protest
against Jewish justice and Roman law,
which had condemned Jesus to death.

It is a protest
against any merely immanent meaning of this world;
with its piety and its laws the world ended up rejecting
    the very person that God now vindicates.
God reveals what true justice is
and unmasks established, official justice.
By his resurrection Jesus gives victory
to the right of the oppressed
and to justice for the weak.
The resurrection will define the import and meaning-
    fulness of our hope.

Why do we die if we yearn to live forever?
What point is there to the death
of those who fall in the struggle for justice?
Who will confer meaning on the spilled blood
of all the nameless people
—peasants, laborers, Indians, and blacks—
who were slain by the powerful simply because they
    sought to stand up for their rights?
Jesus' resurrection answers these inescapable ques-
    tions of the human heart.
Life experiences death,
but it is not swallowed up in death.
It comes through death perfected and triumphant.
Human beings are not born to die;
they die to be resurrected.

The risen Jesus is the convincing confirmation of this
    fact.
Our yearning for human fulfillment
is not frustrated in the end.

The resurrection is the complete and total fulfillment
    of the human being,
body and soul,
within the reality of God's Kingdom.
It is the most significant fact in world history
because it proves that life, not death, has the last word.

The man who was raised up
was not someone with power.
He was a defeated, crucified being.
Through the fate of Jesus,
God has informed us
that the ultimate meaning of history
is turned into a reality
by one who is crucified for identifying himself with
    those who are poor and unjustly treated in this world,
by one who is rejected and cursed for trying to create a
    more fraternal, less evil kind of societal life.
Hence all who work for those causes have a future.
They will enjoy the fulfillment of a resurrected life.
The murderer does not triumph over the victim.
Death, where is your victory?
Oppression, where is your power?

Death has been swallowed up in Christ's resurrection.
Oppression has been transformed into a pathway
to liberation through sacrifice.
The bright rays of new life now penetrate
the dark recesses of the world.
We can now glimpse the first dawning signs
of the new heaven and the new earth.
Amen, alleluia!

This means that if anyone is in Christ,
he is a new creation.
The old order has passed away;
now all is new! (2 Cor. 5:17)

Now:
The resurrection is taking place

The resurrection is not merely a past event,
confined to long ago.
It marks the beginning of the new heaven
and the new earth.
It gives definition to the triumph of life,
which is no longer menaced by death.
Hence it is a perduring present,
a present without end.
The risen Lord continues to live within history.
He is ineffably present in the world,
in each person and in social processes.

The resurrection realizes the utopia of God's King-
    dom—
not universally because of human rejection,
but personally in the destiny of Jesus.
In the person of the risen Jesus
we glimpse what the cosmos and humanity are sum-
    moned to achieve:

complete victory over everything that divides and
    threatens life;
the transfiguration of one's own life,
so that it becomes fully human and fully divine,
fully corporeal and fully spiritual.
God was not defeated
by the ability of human beings to reject him.
He did not give up his plan to establish his Kingdom;
to effect the complete and definitive communion of
    each and all
and thorough reconciliation in a realm
where justice would reign
and brotherhood would cast its warm glow.

Thanks to Jesus' resurrection,
that Kingdom is now a new datum
within the old matter of the world.
It is acting as a leaven everywhere,
helping the dynamisms of life to grow in opposition
to the dynamisms of death.

The Church is the community
of those who join together
to venerate the presence
of the living, resurrected Jesus,
to preserve his memory,
and to live out the commitment to liberation.
As such, it is the privileged bearer of the forces of the
    resurrection.
The Lord is at work in it,
as if it were his own body.
He touches us with his saving gestures
known as the sacraments.

But the risen Jesus
does not confine his activity to the Church.
He penetrates the entire cosmos,
pervades the whole world,
and makes his presence felt in every human being.
The resurrection is a process that began with Jesus
and that will go on until it embraces all creation.
Wherever an authentically human life is growing in the
    world,
wherever justice is triumphing over the instincts of
    domination,
wherever grace is winning out over the power of sin,
wherever human beings are creating more fraternal
    mediations in their social life together,
wherever love is getting the better of selfish interests,
and wherever hope is resisting the lure of cynicism or
    despair,
there the process of resurrection
is being turned into a reality.
It will continue to operate everywhere
until the total transfiguration of the world is achieved
in the definitive parousia of the Lord.

Those who believe in the resurrection
are no longer permitted to live in sadness.
The Way of the Cross,
the painful journey of the Son of God
and his brothers and sisters
through the torments of this world,
does have a real meaning.
We are destined and called to live life to the full:
joyous in our hope,
confident in our love,

and reconciled to the world,
our fellow human beings,
and God.
Thus we already enjoy a foretaste
of the Kingdom's presence
as we anxiously await
the resurrection of the body and eternal life.
Amen.

Photo credits

Other Orbis books . . .

THE MEANING OF MISSION

José Comblin

"This very readable book has made me think, and I feel it will be useful for anyone dealing with their Christian role of mission and evangelism." *New Review of Books and Religion*

ISBN 0-88344-304-X CIP   *Cloth $6.95*

THE GOSPEL OF PEACE AND JUSTICE

Catholic Social Teaching Since Pope John

Presented by Joseph Gremillion

"Especially valuable as a resource. The book brings together 22 documents containing the developing social teaching of the church from *Mater et Magistra* to Pope Paul's 1975 *Peace Day Message on Reconciliation*. I watched the intellectual excitement of students who used Gremillion's book in a justice and peace course I taught last summer, as they discovered a body of teaching on the issues they had defined as relevant. To read Gremillion's overview and prospectus, a meaty introductory essay of some 140 pages, is to be guided through the sea of social teaching by a remarkably adept navigator."

National Catholic Reporter

"An authoritative guide and study aid for concerned Catholics and others." *Library Journal*

ISBN 0-88344-165-9   *Cloth $15.95*
ISBN 0-88344-166-7   *Paper $8.95*

THEOLOGY IN THE AMERICAS

Papers of the 1975 Detroit Conference

Edited by Sergio Torres and John Eagleson

"A pathbreaking book from and about a pathbreaking theological conference, *Theology in the Americas* makes a major contribution to ecumenical theology, Christian social ethics and liberation movements in dialogue." *Fellowship*

ISBN 0-88344-479-8 CIP   *Cloth $12.95*
ISBN 0-88344-476-3   *Paper $5.95*

CHRISTIANS, POLITICS
AND VIOLENT REVOLUTION

J.G. Davies

"Davies argues that violence and revolution are on the agenda the world presents to the Church and that consequently the Church must reflect on such problems. This is a first-rate presentation, with Davies examining the question from every conceivable angle."

National Catholic News Service

ISBN 0-88344-061-X
Paper $4.95

CHRISTIAN POLITICAL THEOLOGY
A MARXIAN GUIDE

Joseph Petulla

"Petulla presents a fresh look at Marxian thought for the benefit of Catholic theologians in the light of the interest in this subject which was spurred by Vatican II, which saw the need for new relationships with men of all political positions." *Journal of Economic Literature*

ISBN 0-88344-060-1
Paper $4.95

THE NEW CREATION:
MARXIST AND CHRISTIAN?

José María González-Ruiz

"A worthy book for lively discussion."

The New Review of Books and Religion

ISBN 0-88344-327-9 CIP
Cloth $6.95

CHRISTIANS AND SOCIALISM

Documentation of the Christians for
Socialism Movement in Latin America

Edited by John Eagleson

"Compelling in its clear presentation of the issue of Christian commitment in a revolutionary world." *The Review of Books and Religion*

ISBN 0-88344-058-X
Paper $4.95

THE CHURCH AND
THIRD WORLD REVOLUTION

Pierre Bigo

"Heavily documented, provocative yet reasonable, this is a testament, demanding but impressive." *Publishers Weekly*

ISBN 0-88344-071-7 CIP   *Cloth $8.95*
ISBN 0-88344-072-5   *Paper $4.95*

WHY IS THE THIRD WORLD POOR?

Piero Gheddo

"An excellent handbook on the Christian understanding of the development process. Gheddo looks at both the internal and external causes of underdevelopment and how Christians can involve themselves in helping the third world." *Provident Book Finder*

ISBN 0-88344-757-6   *Paper $4.95*

POLITICS AND SOCIETY
IN THE THIRD WORLD

Jean-Yves Calvez

"This frank treatment of economic and cultural problems in developing nations suggests the need for constant multiple attacks on the many fronts that produce problems in the human situation."

         The Christian Century
ISBN 0-88344-389-9   *Cloth $6.95*

A THEOLOGY OF LIBERATION

Gustavo Gutiérrez

"The movement's most influential text." *Time*

"The most complete presentation thus far available to English readers of the provocative theology emerging from the Latin American Church." *Theological Studies*

"North Americans as well as Latin Americans will find so many challenges and daring insights that they will, I suggest, rate this book one of the best of its kind ever written." *America*

ISBN 0-88344-477-1   *Cloth $7.95*
ISBN 0-88344-478-X   *Paper $4.95*

THEOLOGY FOR A NOMAD CHURCH

Hugo Assmann

"A new challenge to contemporary theology which attempts to show that the theology of liberation is not just a fad, but a new political dimension which touches every aspect of Christian existence."

Publishers Weekly

ISBN 0-88344-493-3   *Cloth $7.95*
ISBN 0-88344-494-1   *Paper $4.95*

FREEDOM MADE FLESH

The Mission of Christ and His Church

Ignacio Ellacuría

"Ellacuría's main thesis is that God's saving message and revelation are historical, that is, that the proclamation of the gospel message must possess the same historical character that revelation and salvation history do and that, for this reason, it must be carried out in history and in a historical way." *Cross and Crown*

ISBN 0-88344-140-3   *Cloth $8.95*
ISBN 0-88344-141-1   *Paper $4.95*

THE LIBERATION OF THEOLOGY

Juan Luis Segundo

"It is a remarkable book in terms of its boldness in confronting the shortcomings of the Christian tradition and in terms of the clarity of vision provided by the hermeneutic of liberation. Segundo writes with ease whether dealing with the sociological, theological, or political roots of liberation. His is a significant addition to the recent work of Cone, Alves, Moltmann, and Gutiérrez because it compels the movement to interrogate its own theological foundations. A necessary addition, in one of the more fruitful directions of contemporary theology, it is appropriate for graduate, undergraduate, or clerical readers." *Choice*

"The book makes for exciting reading and should not be missing in any theological library." *Library Journal*

ISBN 0-88344-285-X CIP   *Cloth $10.95*
ISBN 0-88344-286-8   *Paper $6.95*

MARX AND THE BIBLE

José Miranda

"An inescapable book which raises more questions than it answers, which will satisfy few of us, but will not let us rest easily again. It is an attempt to utilize the best tradition of Scripture scholarship to understand the text when it is set in a context of human need and misery."
Walter Brueggemann, in Interpretation

ISBN 0-88344-306-6   *Cloth $8.95*
ISBN 0-88344-307-4   *Paper $4.95*

BEING AND THE MESSIAH

The Message of Saint John

José Miranda

"This book could become the catalyst of a new debate on the Fourth Gospel. Johannine scholarship will hotly debate the 'terrifyingly revolutionary thesis that this world of contempt and oppression can be changed into a world of complete selflessness and unrestricted mutual assistance.' Cast in the framework of an analysis of contemporary philosophy, the volume will prove a classic of Latin American theology." *Frederick Herzog, Duke University Divinity School*

ISBN 0-88344-027-X CIP   *Cloth $8.95*
ISBN 0-88344-028-8   *Paper $4.95*

THE GOSPEL IN SOLENTINAME

Ernesto Cardenal

"Upon reading this book, I want to do so many things—burn all my other books which at best seem like hay, soggy with mildew. I now know who (not what) is the church and how to celebrate church in the eucharist. The dialogues are intense, profound, radical. *The Gospel in Solentiname* calls us home."
Carroll Stuhlmueller, National Catholic Reporter

ISBN 0-88344-168-3   *Vol. 1 Cloth $6.95*
ISBN 0-88344-170-5   *Vol. 1 Paper $4.95*
ISBN 0-88344-167-5   *Vol. 2 Cloth $6.95*

THE CHURCH AND POWER IN BRAZIL

Charles Antoine

"This is a book which should serve as a basis of discussion and further study by all who are interested in the relationship of the Church to contemporary governments, and all who believe that the Church has a vital role to play in the quest for social justice." *Worldmission*
ISBN 0-88344-062-8   *Paper $4.95*

HISTORY AND
THE THEOLOGY OF LIBERATION

Enrique Dussel

"The book is easy reading. It is a brilliant study of what may well be or should be the future course of theological methodology."
Religious Media Today
ISBN 0-88344-179-9   *Cloth $8.95*
ISBN 0-88344-180-2   *Paper $4.95*

DOM HELDER CAMARA

José de Broucker

"De Broucker, an internationally recognized journalist, develops a portrait, at once intimate, comprehensive and sympathetic, of the Archbishop of Olinda and Recife, Brazil, whose championship of political and economic justice for the hungry, unorganized masses of his country and all Latin America has aroused world attention."
America
ISBN 0-88344-099-7   *Cloth $6.95*

THE DESERT IS FERTILE

Dom Helder Camara

"Camara's brief essays and poems are arresting for their simplicity and depth of vision, and are encouraging because of the realistic yet quietly hopeful tone with which they argue for sustained action toward global justice." *Commonweal*
ISBN 0-88344-078-4   *Cloth $3.95*